The Adventures of Shoofully

The adventures of Shoofully is an easy-to-read, fun, and educational book series for kids that is meant to get your child excited about reading and learning all while having fun. This is the 1st book of the series of 10.

Shoofully the cutest little dog has just been born. He has puffy eyes, an adorable nose, and a wagging tail and is coming to your homes to touch your hearts. Follow him to the next book to find out about all the fun things that he is going to discover.

COPYRIGHT 2021 by Sunshine Creations. All rights reserved.

Written and Published By: Sunshine Creations
Illustrated By: Ali Pourazar

Shoofully The Wonder Dog

I didn't have to open my eyes to know that the best mommy in the world was next to me. When I opened them and I saw her, I had a big smile on my face. She was everything I would ever need. I was happy and thankful that she was by my side.

Her fur was soft, and her milk tasted so good! If this is what the rest of my life is going to be like, I'm sold! Sign me up for more!

I'm only a few days old now, but my mommy says that I'm a handful already.
Mommy and my siblings call me Shoofully!
I guess that's my name.

Sometimes mommy licks my shaggy brown fur, even when I think I don't need it. But you know what? She is always right! Her licking calms me down so I don't get too afraid of this giant new world and all the new things in it.

Sometimes she licks the white heart-shaped spot on my snout, which always makes me sneeze. Like now... [sneezes].

There is one thing I almost love as much as my mommy and her milk: my blankie. I call it Fuzzy. Fuzzy is purple and green and is so warm. It smells like my mommy and my siblings. Mommy says I should not tinkle on the fuzzy, because then it will be smelly and uncomfortable. But I sometimes get too excited, and I pee just a little bit.

We live in a house with another family. They don't look like us. Mommy says that they are called humans. They take good care of us. One of the humans washed my blankie today. I think she is also a mommy and takes care of the little humans in this house. Fuzzy is as good as new and I'm so happy.

One day I woke up and one of my siblings was not in our box. I looked for her everywhere. I checked under mommy's belly, looked behind mommy, and even on top of mommy.

I woke up all my siblings and we all started searching the box, but my sister was not there!

We made so much noise that we woke up mommy. She gathered us all up and said that there are some other humans in the world who don't live in our house. They might be lonely or sad or they might just need to give love to a puppy. So sometimes we go with them to their houses to take care of them and they take care of us.

My siblings and I are still a little confused but at least now we know that our sister is safe, and she is with a new family.

I am proud of my sister and super excited for her. She has gone to make a new family happy. One day I will have the chance to do that too.

Mommy says, even though I'm so little, I can make a big difference and make people happy. I can take away their sadness and make this world a better place.

That's a big Job!

Some days I miss my sister. She used to yip all the time, but she was so fun to play with. We used to sit beside each other at mommy's pumping station, and we used to race to drink mommy's milk. Sometimes she won and sometimes I did. I will never forget her, and I will love her forever.

I spent the next few days thinking about my sister and how she was out there in this giant world doing big things. I might've looked sad because the human mommy kept hugging me! But I was mostly thinking about all the big things I wanted to do one day. A couple of days later, something happened that made me really excited.....

Follow us on Facebook or Instagram to find out what happens to Shoofully next!
You will be the first to know when the next book is ready to be published.

Check us out in Instagram and Facebook:

 Facebook.com/sunshinecreations555

 Instegram.com/sunshinecreations555

Email us at: sunshinecreations555@Gmail.com

Check out the book#2 in my Amazon author page

amazon.com/author/sunshinecreations555

www.ingramcontent.com/pod-product-compliance
Lightning Source LLC
Chambersburg PA
CBHW051307110526
44589CB00025B/2962